The Litify System Administrator's Guide For Paralegals and Non-Technical Personnel

Written By Richard Aragon

Table of Contents

Chapter 1: Getting Started with Litify

Introduction

Welcome to the Litify System Administrator Guide! This guide is designed to help paralegals and other legal professionals with little to no technical experience become proficient in using Litify. Litify is a powerful, cloud-based platform built on Salesforce that combines case management, document management, and client communication tools into a single, integrated solution. Let's begin by understanding the basics of Litify and how to get started with the platform.

What is Litify?

Litify is a comprehensive legal practice management platform designed to streamline and enhance the efficiency of law firms. It integrates various tools and features to manage cases, documents, and client communications, all within the Salesforce ecosystem. Here are some of the core components of Litify:

- **Docrio:** A document management system that allows for easy creation, storage, and sharing of legal documents.
- **Case Management:** Tools to track case progress, manage tasks, and collaborate with team members.
- **Client Communication:** Features for logging and managing client interactions.

Logging In

To get started with Litify, you need to log into the platform. Follow these steps:

1. **Open Your Web Browser:** Litify is a cloud-based platform, so you can access it through any modern web browser such as Google Chrome, Firefox, or Safari.
2. **Go to the Login Page:** Navigate to the Litify login page provided by your firm. This is typically a unique URL assigned to your organization.
3. **Enter Your Credentials:** Use your assigned username and password to log in. If you do not have login credentials, contact your system administrator or IT department for assistance.

Navigating the Litify Interface

Once you are logged in, you will see the Litify dashboard. The dashboard is your central hub for accessing all the features and tools available in Litify. Here are some key elements of the interface:

- **Navigation Bar:** Located at the top of the screen, the navigation bar provides access to different sections such as Cases, Documents, Tasks, and Contacts.

- **Search Bar:** Use the search bar to quickly find cases, documents, or contacts by typing in keywords or names.
- **Dashboard Widgets:** These are customizable elements on your dashboard that provide quick access to important information and frequently used tools.

Basic Settings and Customization

To ensure that Litify works best for you, it's important to customize some basic settings:

1. **Profile Settings:** Click on your profile icon in the top right corner of the screen and select "Settings." Here you can update your personal information, change your password, and set preferences such as notification settings.
2. **Dashboard Customization:** Customize your dashboard by adding or removing widgets. Click the "Edit" button on the dashboard to modify the layout and select the widgets that are most useful for your daily tasks.
3. **Email Integration:** Integrate your email account with Litify to ensure all client communications are logged and accessible within the platform. Follow the prompts in the email integration settings to connect your email account.

Understanding Key Features

Litify offers a wide range of features designed to simplify your workflow. Here are some of the essential features you will use frequently:

- **Case Management:** Track the progress of your cases, assign tasks to team members, and set deadlines. Use the case timeline to see a chronological view of all activities related to a case.
- **Document Management (Docrio):** Create, store, and share documents within the platform. Use the document templates to quickly generate common legal documents and the bulk upload feature to add multiple files at once.
- **Task Management:** Create and assign tasks to yourself or other team members. Set due dates and priorities to ensure that important tasks are completed on time.
- **Client Communication:** Log all client interactions, including emails and phone calls, within Litify. Use the communication tools to send and receive messages directly from the platform.

Getting Help

As you start using Litify, you may have questions or need assistance. Here are some resources to help you:

- **Help Center:** Access the Litify Help Center from the navigation bar. It contains a wealth of articles, tutorials, and FAQs to help you understand and use the platform.
- **Support Team:** Contact the Litify support team for assistance with technical issues or questions. You can usually reach them via email or through the support portal.

- **Training Resources:** Litify offers training sessions and webinars to help users get the most out of the platform. Check the training schedule and sign up for sessions that interest you.

Conclusion

Congratulations on completing Chapter 1 of the Litify System Administrator Guide! By now, you should have a basic understanding of what Litify is, how to log in, navigate the interface, customize settings, and utilize key features. In the next chapter, we will dive deeper into case management and explore how to manage cases effectively within Litify. Happy learning!

Chapter 2: Managing Cases in Litify

Introduction

Welcome to Chapter 2 of the Litify System Administrator Guide! In this chapter, we will delve into the case management features of Litify. Managing cases effectively is crucial for any law firm, and Litify offers a range of tools to help you track, organize, and collaborate on cases. By the end of this chapter, you will have a solid understanding of how to create, manage, and track cases within Litify.

Creating a New Case

Creating a new case in Litify is straightforward. Follow these steps to get started:

1. **Navigate to the Cases Tab:**
   - From the navigation bar, click on the "Cases" tab. This will take you to the case management section.
2. **Click on "New Case":**
   - In the Cases tab, you will see a "New Case" button. Click on it to open the case creation form.
3. **Fill in Case Details:**
   - Enter the relevant information for the new case, including the case name, type, client details, and any other pertinent information. Make sure to fill out all mandatory fields marked with an asterisk (*).
4. **Assign Team Members:**
   - Assign the case to team members by selecting their names from the dropdown menu. You can also set their roles and responsibilities within the case.
5. **Save the Case:**
   - Once you have filled in all the necessary information, click the "Save" button to create the case. The new case will now appear in the Cases tab.

Organizing Case Information

Litify allows you to organize and categorize case information efficiently. Here are some key features to help you stay organized:

1. **Case Timelines:**
   - The case timeline provides a chronological view of all activities related to the case. This includes emails, notes, documents, and tasks. You can filter the timeline to view specific types of activities.
2. **Case Stages:**
   - Litify allows you to define and track the stages of a case. For example, stages might include "Intake," "Discovery," "Litigation," and "Resolution." You can move cases through these stages to reflect their current status.

3. **Tags and Categories:**
   - Use tags and categories to label and organize cases. This makes it easier to search for and filter cases based on specific criteria.
4. **Related Records:**
   - Link related records such as contacts, documents, and tasks to a case. This provides a comprehensive view of all information related to the case in one place.

Tracking Case Progress

Monitoring the progress of cases is essential to ensure timely and successful outcomes. Litify provides several tools to help you track case progress:

1. **Case Dashboard:**
   - The case dashboard gives you a quick overview of all your active cases, including their current stage, assigned team members, and upcoming deadlines. You can customize the dashboard to display the information most relevant to you.
2. **Tasks and Deadlines:**
   - Create and assign tasks to team members, set due dates, and track their completion. Use the calendar view to see all upcoming deadlines and ensure that nothing falls through the cracks.
3. **Activity Logs:**
   - The activity log tracks all actions taken on a case, such as emails sent, documents uploaded, and tasks completed. This helps you maintain an accurate record of case activities.
4. **Reports and Analytics:**
   - Generate reports to analyze case performance, track key metrics, and identify areas for improvement. Litify's reporting tools allow you to create custom reports based on your specific needs.

Collaborating with Team Members

Effective collaboration is crucial for managing cases successfully. Litify offers several features to facilitate teamwork:

1. **Shared Notes:**
   - Use shared notes to document important case information and updates. Team members can add comments and collaborate in real-time.
2. **Document Sharing:**
   - Upload and share documents related to the case with your team. Use the document management features to organize, categorize, and version-control documents.
3. **Communication Tools:**
   - Log all client communications, including emails and phone calls, within Litify. Use the built-in messaging tools to communicate with team members without leaving the platform.

Best Practices for Case Management

To make the most of Litify's case management features, consider the following best practices:

1. **Consistent Data Entry:**
   - Ensure that all team members follow consistent data entry practices. This helps maintain accurate and organized case records.
2. **Regular Updates:**
   - Regularly update case information, including status changes, new tasks, and completed activities. This keeps everyone on the same page and ensures that nothing is overlooked.
3. **Use Templates:**
   - Utilize templates for common documents and communications. This saves time and ensures consistency across all cases.
4. **Monitor Performance:**
   - Use Litify's reporting and analytics tools to monitor case performance and identify trends. This helps you make informed decisions and improve your firm's efficiency.

Conclusion

Congratulations on completing Chapter 2 of the Litify System Administrator Guide! You now have a solid understanding of how to create, organize, and track cases within Litify. In the next chapter, we will explore document management in detail, including how to create, store, and share documents using Docrio. Happy case managing!

Chapter 3: Document Management with Docrio

Introduction

Welcome to Chapter 3 of the Litify System Administrator Guide! In this chapter, we will focus on Docrio, Litify's powerful document management system. Docrio allows you to create, store, organize, and share documents efficiently within your law firm. By the end of this chapter, you will understand how to utilize Docrio to manage documents effectively, ensuring that all your legal documents are easily accessible and securely managed.

Overview of Docrio

Docrio is designed to streamline the document management process for law firms. It integrates seamlessly with Litify and Salesforce, providing a centralized location for all your documents. Here are some key features of Docrio:

- **Document Creation:** Use templates to generate new documents quickly and consistently.
- **Storage and Organization:** Store documents in case-specific folders and categorize them for easy retrieval.
- **Version Control:** Track changes and maintain multiple versions of documents.
- **Secure Sharing:** Share documents securely within your organization and with external parties.

Creating Documents

Creating documents in Docrio is straightforward. Follow these steps to create a new document:

1. **Navigate to the Documents Tab:**
   - From the navigation bar, click on the "Documents" tab to open the document management section.
2. **Click on "New Document":**
   - In the Documents tab, click the "New Document" button. This will open the document creation form.
3. **Select a Template:**
   - Choose a template from the list of available templates. Templates help ensure consistency and save time by pre-populating standard information.
4. **Fill in Document Details:**
   - Enter the necessary details for the document, such as client information, case details, and any specific content required.
5. **Save the Document:**
   - Once you have completed the document, click the "Save" button. The document will be stored in the appropriate case folder and categorized accordingly.

Storing and Organizing Documents

Docrio provides several tools to help you store and organize documents effectively:

1. **Case-Specific Folders:**
   - Documents are stored in case-specific folders, making it easy to find all documents related to a particular case. Navigate to the case folder to view all associated documents.
2. **Categorization:**
   - Categorize documents using tags and categories. This helps in quickly retrieving documents based on specific criteria, such as document type or date.
3. **Bulk Upload:**
   - Use the bulk upload feature to upload multiple documents at once. This is particularly useful when dealing with large volumes of documents.
4. **Search and Filters:**
   - Utilize the search bar and filters to find documents quickly. You can search by document name, category, date, or other metadata.

Version Control

Docrio's version control feature allows you to track changes and maintain multiple versions of documents. Here's how to manage document versions:

1. **Editing Documents:**
   - Open the document you wish to edit and make the necessary changes. Each time you save the document, a new version is created.
2. **Viewing Version History:**
   - Click on the document's "Version History" tab to view all previous versions. This allows you to track changes and revert to an earlier version if needed.
3. **Comparing Versions:**
   - Use the version comparison tool to see the differences between two versions of a document. This is useful for identifying changes and ensuring accuracy.

Secure Sharing

Docrio makes it easy to share documents securely within your organization and with external parties:

1. **Internal Sharing:**
   - Share documents with colleagues by setting access permissions. You can specify who can view, edit, or comment on a document.
2. **External Sharing:**
   - Use secure links to share documents with external parties. You can set expiration dates for the links and require passwords for added security.
3. **Tracking Access:**

- Monitor who has accessed a shared document and what actions they have taken. This helps maintain control over document security and confidentiality.

Best Practices for Document Management

To make the most of Docrio, consider the following best practices:

1. **Consistent Naming Conventions:**
   - Use consistent naming conventions for documents to make them easier to find and organize.
2. **Regular Backups:**
   - Regularly back up your documents to ensure that you do not lose important information in case of a system failure.
3. **Access Control:**
   - Implement strict access controls to ensure that only authorized personnel can view or edit sensitive documents.
4. **Training:**
   - Provide training to all users on how to use Docrio effectively. This ensures that everyone is familiar with the system and can use it to its full potential.

Conclusion

Congratulations on completing Chapter 3 of the Litify System Administrator Guide! You now have a thorough understanding of how to use Docrio for document management. In the next chapter, we will explore client communication tools and how to manage interactions with clients effectively within Litify. Happy document managing!

Chapter 4: Managing Client Communications in Litify

Introduction

Welcome to Chapter 4 of the Litify System Administrator Guide! In this chapter, we will focus on managing client communications within Litify. Effective communication with clients is essential for any law firm, and Litify offers a range of tools to help you log, track, and manage all interactions. By the end of this chapter, you will understand how to use these tools to ensure clear, consistent, and professional communication with your clients.

Overview of Client Communication Tools

Litify provides several features designed to streamline client communications. These include email logging, phone call tracking, and integrated messaging tools. Here are some of the key components:

- **Email Logging:** Automatically log emails to ensure all client communications are recorded.
- **Phone Call Tracking:** Log and track phone calls with clients, including call details and outcomes.
- **Messaging Tools:** Use integrated messaging tools to communicate with clients and team members directly within the platform.

Setting Up Email Integration

To manage client emails within Litify, you need to integrate your email account. Here's how to set up email integration:

1. **Navigate to Email Settings:**
   - Click on your profile icon in the top right corner and select "Settings." Then, navigate to the "Email Integration" section.
2. **Connect Your Email Account:**
   - Follow the prompts to connect your email account. You will need to enter your email address and password, and grant Litify permission to access your emails.
3. **Configure Email Logging:**
   - Set up email logging preferences. You can choose to log all emails automatically or manually select which emails to log. Make sure to configure these settings according to your firm's policies.

Logging and Tracking Emails

Once your email account is integrated, you can start logging and tracking emails. Here's how:

1. **Compose and Send Emails:**

- Compose emails directly within Litify or your email client. If you have set up automatic logging, these emails will be logged in the relevant case or contact record.

2. **Manually Log Emails:**
   - To manually log an email, navigate to the relevant case or contact record, and click on the "Emails" tab. Select "Log Email" and fill in the email details.

3. **Viewing Logged Emails:**
   - All logged emails can be viewed under the "Emails" tab in the relevant case or contact record. This provides a complete history of email communications.

Tracking Phone Calls

Logging phone calls ensures that all verbal communications with clients are recorded. Follow these steps to log and track phone calls:

1. **Log a New Call:**
   - Navigate to the relevant case or contact record and click on the "Calls" tab. Select "Log Call" and fill in the call details, including the date, time, duration, and call summary.

2. **Track Call Outcomes:**
   - Record the outcome of the call, such as "Follow-up Required," "Message Left," or "Issue Resolved." This helps in tracking the status of each client interaction.

3. **Viewing Call Logs:**
   - All logged calls can be viewed under the "Calls" tab in the relevant case or contact record. This provides a complete history of phone communications.

Using Messaging Tools

Litify's integrated messaging tools allow you to communicate with clients and team members directly within the platform. Here's how to use these tools:

1. **Send a Message:**
   - Navigate to the relevant case or contact record and click on the "Messages" tab. Select "New Message" and compose your message. You can send messages to clients or internal team members.

2. **View Message History:**
   - All sent and received messages can be viewed under the "Messages" tab in the relevant case or contact record. This provides a complete history of written communications.

3. **Set Up Notifications:**
   - Configure notification settings to receive alerts for new messages. This ensures that you stay informed about all client communications.

Best Practices for Client Communications

To ensure effective and professional client communications, consider the following best practices:

1. **Consistent Communication:**
   - Maintain regular and consistent communication with clients. Update them on case progress and respond promptly to their inquiries.
2. **Clear and Concise Messaging:**
   - Keep your messages clear and concise. Avoid using legal jargon and ensure that clients understand the information you provide.
3. **Document Everything:**
   - Log all communications, including emails, phone calls, and messages. This ensures a complete record of all interactions and helps in case of disputes or misunderstandings.
4. **Use Templates:**
   - Utilize email and message templates for common communications. This saves time and ensures consistency in your messaging.

Conclusion

Congratulations on completing Chapter 4 of the Litify System Administrator Guide! You now have a thorough understanding of how to manage client communications within Litify. By utilizing the email logging, phone call tracking, and messaging tools, you can ensure clear, consistent, and professional communication with your clients. In the next chapter, we will explore the reporting and analytics features of Litify, helping you to monitor performance and make data-driven decisions. Happy communicating!

Chapter 5: Reporting and Analytics in Litify

Introduction

Welcome to Chapter 5 of the Litify System Administrator Guide! In this chapter, we will explore the reporting and analytics features of Litify. These tools are essential for monitoring your firm's performance, tracking key metrics, and making data-driven decisions. By the end of this chapter, you will understand how to create, customize, and interpret reports to gain valuable insights into your firm's operations.

Overview of Reporting and Analytics

Litify's reporting and analytics tools are built on the Salesforce platform, providing robust capabilities to generate and analyze data. Key features include:

- **Pre-built Reports:** Ready-made reports that cover common metrics and KPIs.
- **Custom Reports:** Ability to create reports tailored to your specific needs.
- **Dashboards:** Visual representations of key metrics, offering a quick overview of performance.
- **Analytics Tools:** Advanced tools to drill down into data and uncover insights.

Accessing Reports

To get started with reports in Litify, follow these steps:

1. **Navigate to the Reports Tab:**
    - From the navigation bar, click on the "Reports" tab. This will take you to the reports section.
2. **Explore Pre-built Reports:**
    - Litify offers a variety of pre-built reports that cover common metrics such as case status, task completion, and financial performance. Browse through these reports to see if any meet your needs.
3. **Running a Report:**
    - Select a report from the list and click "Run Report." This will generate the report based on the most current data.

Creating Custom Reports

If the pre-built reports do not cover your specific needs, you can create custom reports. Here's how:

1. **Click on "New Report":**
    - In the Reports tab, click the "New Report" button. This will open the report builder interface.

2. **Choose a Report Type:**
   - Select the type of report you want to create based on the data you need. Common report types include cases, tasks, and financials.
3. **Add Filters:**
   - Use filters to narrow down the data included in your report. For example, you might filter cases by status, date range, or assigned team member.
4. **Select Fields:**
   - Choose the fields you want to include in your report. These might include case name, client name, task completion date, and more.
5. **Generate the Report:**
   - Once you have configured the filters and fields, click "Generate Report" to create your custom report. You can then save the report for future use.

Creating Dashboards

Dashboards provide a visual representation of key metrics, making it easy to monitor performance at a glance. Here's how to create a dashboard:

1. **Navigate to the Dashboards Tab:**
   - From the navigation bar, click on the "Dashboards" tab.
2. **Click on "New Dashboard":**
   - Click the "New Dashboard" button to create a new dashboard.
3. **Add Components:**
   - Add components to your dashboard, such as charts, graphs, and tables. Each component represents a specific metric or KPI.
4. **Customize Layout:**
   - Arrange the components on your dashboard to create a layout that suits your needs. You can resize and move components as needed.
5. **Save and Share:**
   - Save your dashboard and share it with team members. You can also set up scheduled refreshes to ensure the data is always up-to-date.

Using Analytics Tools

Litify's analytics tools allow you to delve deeper into your data to uncover insights and trends. Here are some key tools:

1. **Drill-Down Analysis:**
   - Use drill-down analysis to explore the details behind your metrics. For example, if you see a spike in case closures, drill down to see which cases contributed to the spike.
2. **Trend Analysis:**
   - Analyze trends over time to identify patterns and predict future performance. This can help you make informed decisions about resource allocation and strategy.
3. **Comparative Analysis:**

- Compare different data sets to identify correlations and insights. For example, compare task completion rates across different teams to see which team is the most efficient.

Best Practices for Reporting and Analytics

To make the most of Litify's reporting and analytics features, consider the following best practices:

1. **Regular Monitoring:**
   - Regularly monitor key metrics and reports to stay informed about your firm's performance. Set up scheduled reports and dashboard refreshes to keep data current.
2. **Actionable Insights:**
   - Focus on generating reports that provide actionable insights. Avoid overwhelming yourself with data; instead, identify key metrics that drive decision-making.
3. **Data Accuracy:**
   - Ensure that the data entered into Litify is accurate and up-to-date. Inaccurate data can lead to misleading reports and poor decision-making.
4. **Training:**
   - Provide training to team members on how to create and interpret reports. This ensures that everyone can leverage the power of reporting and analytics.

Conclusion

Congratulations on completing Chapter 5 of the Litify System Administrator Guide! You now have a comprehensive understanding of how to use Litify's reporting and analytics tools to monitor performance and make data-driven decisions. In the next chapter, we will explore task and calendar management, helping you to stay organized and on top of your responsibilities. Happy analyzing!

Chapter 6: Task and Calendar Management in Litify

Introduction

Welcome to Chapter 6 of the Litify System Administrator Guide! In this chapter, we will focus on task and calendar management within Litify. Efficiently managing tasks and calendars is essential for keeping track of deadlines, appointments, and responsibilities. By the end of this chapter, you will understand how to use Litify's task and calendar management tools to stay organized and ensure that nothing falls through the cracks.

Overview of Task and Calendar Management

Litify offers robust tools for managing tasks and calendars, helping you to keep track of your daily responsibilities and long-term projects. Key features include:

- **Task Creation and Assignment:** Create and assign tasks to yourself or team members.
- **Task Tracking:** Monitor the progress of tasks and ensure they are completed on time.
- **Calendar Integration:** Sync your tasks and appointments with your calendar to have a unified view of your schedule.
- **Reminders and Notifications:** Set reminders and notifications to stay on top of important deadlines.

Creating and Assigning Tasks

Creating and assigning tasks in Litify is straightforward. Follow these steps to get started:

1. **Navigate to the Tasks Tab:**
   - From the navigation bar, click on the "Tasks" tab to open the task management section.
2. **Click on "New Task":**
   - In the Tasks tab, click the "New Task" button to open the task creation form.
3. **Enter Task Details:**
   - Fill in the task details, including the task name, description, due date, priority, and any relevant notes.
4. **Assign the Task:**
   - Assign the task to yourself or another team member by selecting their name from the dropdown menu. You can also set the task's status and due date.
5. **Save the Task:**
   - Once you have entered all the necessary information, click the "Save" button to create the task. The task will now appear in the Tasks tab and on the assigned user's dashboard.

Tracking and Managing Tasks

Once tasks are created and assigned, it's important to track their progress and ensure they are completed on time. Here's how to manage tasks effectively:

1. **Task List View:**
   o The Tasks tab provides a list view of all tasks, showing key details such as task name, assignee, due date, and status. Use this view to get a quick overview of all pending tasks.
2. **Task Filters:**
   o Use filters to narrow down the task list based on criteria such as due date, priority, and status. This helps you focus on the most urgent and important tasks.
3. **Updating Task Status:**
   o As tasks are completed, update their status by clicking on the task and selecting the appropriate status (e.g., In Progress, Completed, On Hold).
4. **Task Notifications:**
   o Set up notifications to receive alerts for upcoming tasks and deadlines. This ensures that you stay on top of your responsibilities.

Calendar Integration

Litify's calendar integration allows you to sync tasks and appointments with your calendar. Here's how to make the most of this feature:

1. **Access the Calendar:**
   o From the navigation bar, click on the "Calendar" tab to open the calendar view.
2. **Adding Appointments:**
   o Click on a date in the calendar to add a new appointment. Enter the appointment details, including title, description, date, time, and any attendees.
3. **Syncing Tasks:**
   o Tasks with due dates will automatically appear in your calendar. This provides a unified view of your schedule, combining tasks and appointments.
4. **Setting Reminders:**
   o Set reminders for appointments and tasks to receive notifications before they are due. This helps ensure that you are prepared for upcoming events.

Best Practices for Task and Calendar Management

To make the most of Litify's task and calendar management features, consider the following best practices:

1. **Prioritize Tasks:**
   o Prioritize tasks based on their importance and urgency. Focus on high-priority tasks first to ensure that critical deadlines are met.
2. **Regularly Review Tasks and Calendar:**

- Regularly review your task list and calendar to stay updated on your responsibilities. Make adjustments as needed to accommodate new tasks and appointments.
3. **Set Realistic Deadlines:**
   - Set realistic deadlines for tasks and appointments. Avoid overloading yourself or your team with too many tasks at once.
4. **Communicate with Team Members:**
   - Maintain open communication with team members regarding task assignments and deadlines. This helps ensure that everyone is on the same page and working towards common goals.
5. **Utilize Recurring Tasks:**
   - For tasks that occur regularly, set them up as recurring tasks. This saves time and ensures that routine tasks are not overlooked.

Conclusion

Congratulations on completing Chapter 6 of the Litify System Administrator Guide! You now have a thorough understanding of how to manage tasks and calendars within Litify. By utilizing these tools effectively, you can stay organized, meet deadlines, and ensure that all responsibilities are handled efficiently. In the next chapter, we will explore user management and permissions, helping you to control access and maintain security within the Litify platform. Happy task managing!

Chapter 7: User Management and Permissions in Litify

Introduction

Welcome to Chapter 7 of the Litify System Administrator Guide! In this chapter, we will focus on user management and permissions. Managing users and their permissions is crucial to maintaining security and ensuring that everyone has the appropriate access to the tools and information they need. By the end of this chapter, you will understand how to create and manage user accounts, assign roles, and configure permissions within Litify.

Overview of User Management and Permissions

Litify, built on Salesforce, provides robust user management and permission features to help you control access and maintain security. Key components include:

- **User Accounts:** Creating and managing user accounts.
- **Roles and Profiles:** Assigning roles and profiles to define access levels and permissions.
- **Permission Sets:** Customizing permissions for specific users or groups.
- **Security Settings:** Configuring security settings to protect sensitive information.

Creating and Managing User Accounts

To start managing users in Litify, follow these steps:

1. **Navigate to the Users Tab:**
   - From the navigation bar, click on the "Setup" icon (usually a gear symbol) and select "Users" under the Administration section.
2. **Create a New User:**
   - Click on the "New User" button to open the user creation form.
3. **Enter User Details:**
   - Fill in the user details, including name, email address, username, and other required information. Make sure to choose a unique username and set a temporary password.
4. **Assign a Role:**
   - Select a role for the user from the dropdown menu. Roles determine the user's access level and hierarchy within the organization.
5. **Assign a Profile:**
   - Choose a profile for the user. Profiles define the baseline permissions for what users can do within Litify.
6. **Save the User:**
   - Once you have entered all the necessary information, click the "Save" button to create the user account. The new user will receive an email with login instructions.

Assigning Roles and Profiles

Roles and profiles are essential for defining access levels and permissions within Litify. Here's how to assign and manage them:

1. **Understanding Roles:**
   - Roles determine the user's position in the organizational hierarchy and influence data visibility. Users can only see data that their role and hierarchy level permit.
2. **Assigning Roles:**
   - When creating or editing a user account, select the appropriate role from the dropdown menu. You can create custom roles based on your firm's structure and needs.
3. **Understanding Profiles:**
   - Profiles define what users can do within Litify, such as creating or editing records, running reports, and accessing specific features.
4. **Assigning Profiles:**
   - Choose a profile for each user that matches their job responsibilities. Standard profiles include System Administrator, Standard User, and Read-Only User. You can also create custom profiles for more granular control.

Configuring Permission Sets

Permission sets allow you to grant additional permissions to specific users without changing their profiles. Here's how to use permission sets:

1. **Navigate to Permission Sets:**
   - From the Setup menu, select "Permission Sets" under the Users section.
2. **Create a New Permission Set:**
   - Click on the "New Permission Set" button to create a custom permission set.
3. **Define Permissions:**
   - Set the specific permissions you want to grant, such as access to certain objects, fields, or applications.
4. **Assign Permission Sets:**
   - Assign the permission set to individual users or groups of users who need the additional permissions. This is done through the "Manage Assignments" button within the permission set.

Security Settings

To maintain the security of your Litify environment, configure the following security settings:

1. **Password Policies:**
   - Set strong password policies to ensure that all users use secure passwords. This includes requirements for password length, complexity, and expiration.
2. **Login Access Policies:**

- o Define login access policies, such as IP restrictions and login hours, to control when and where users can access the system.
3. **Two-Factor Authentication (2FA):**
   - o Enable two-factor authentication for added security. This requires users to provide a second form of verification, such as a code sent to their phone, when logging in.
4. **Audit Logs:**
   - o Regularly review audit logs to monitor user activity and identify any unauthorized access or unusual behavior.

Best Practices for User Management and Permissions

To effectively manage users and permissions in Litify, consider the following best practices:

1. **Regularly Review User Access:**
   - o Periodically review user roles, profiles, and permission sets to ensure that access levels are appropriate and up-to-date.
2. **Implement the Principle of Least Privilege:**
   - o Grant users the minimum level of access necessary for their job functions. This reduces the risk of unauthorized access to sensitive information.
3. **Conduct Security Training:**
   - o Provide training for all users on security best practices, including password management, recognizing phishing attempts, and safe data handling.
4. **Use Permission Sets Sparingly:**
   - o While permission sets are useful for granting additional access, use them sparingly to avoid overly complex permission configurations.

Conclusion

Congratulations on completing Chapter 7 of the Litify System Administrator Guide! You now have a comprehensive understanding of user management and permissions within Litify. By effectively managing user accounts, roles, profiles, and permissions, you can maintain security and ensure that everyone has the appropriate access to the tools and information they need. In the next chapter, we will explore workflow automation, helping you to streamline processes and improve efficiency within your firm. Happy user managing!

Chapter 8: Workflow Automation in Litify

Introduction

Welcome to Chapter 8 of the Litify System Administrator Guide! In this chapter, we will explore workflow automation within Litify. Automating workflows can help streamline your firm's processes, reduce manual tasks, and improve overall efficiency. By the end of this chapter, you will understand how to create and manage automated workflows using Litify's tools, ensuring that your firm operates smoothly and effectively.

Overview of Workflow Automation

Workflow automation in Litify leverages the power of Salesforce's automation tools to create streamlined processes. Key components of workflow automation include:

- **Process Builder:** A visual tool to automate business processes.
- **Workflow Rules:** Define criteria and actions for automating tasks.
- **Approval Processes:** Automate the routing and approval of records.
- **Flow Builder:** Create more complex automations with conditional logic and user interactions.

Using Process Builder

Process Builder is a powerful tool for automating business processes using a visual interface. Here's how to use it:

1. **Navigate to Process Builder:**
   - From the Setup menu, type "Process Builder" in the Quick Find box and select it.
2. **Create a New Process:**
   - Click on the "New" button to create a new process. Name your process and define when it should start (e.g., when a record is created or edited).
3. **Define Criteria:**
   - Set criteria to determine when the process should run. For example, you can specify that the process runs when a case is assigned to a particular user or when a task is marked as completed.
4. **Add Actions:**
   - Define actions that should be taken when the criteria are met. Actions can include creating records, updating fields, sending emails, and more.
5. **Activate the Process:**
   - Once you have configured the criteria and actions, activate the process to start automating your workflows.

Creating Workflow Rules

Workflow rules are another method to automate tasks based on specific criteria. Here's how to create and manage workflow rules:

1. **Navigate to Workflow Rules:**
   - From the Setup menu, type "Workflow Rules" in the Quick Find box and select it.
2. **Create a New Rule:**
   - Click on the "New Rule" button and select the object you want the rule to apply to (e.g., Cases, Tasks).
3. **Define Criteria:**
   - Set the criteria that will trigger the rule. For example, you might create a rule that triggers when a case status is changed to "Closed."
4. **Add Actions:**
   - Specify the actions that should be taken when the rule criteria are met. Actions can include field updates, email alerts, task creation, and outbound messages.
5. **Activate the Rule:**
   - Save and activate the workflow rule to put it into effect.

Setting Up Approval Processes

Approval processes help automate the routing and approval of records within your firm. Here's how to set up an approval process:

1. **Navigate to Approval Processes:**
   - From the Setup menu, type "Approval Processes" in the Quick Find box and select it.
2. **Create a New Approval Process:**
   - Click on the "Create New Approval Process" button and follow the wizard to set up your process.
3. **Define Entry Criteria:**
   - Set the criteria that records must meet to enter the approval process. For example, you might require that all expense reports over a certain amount be approved.
4. **Specify Approval Steps:**
   - Define the steps in the approval process, including who needs to approve the records at each step.
5. **Configure Actions:**
   - Set up actions to be taken at each step, such as email notifications to approvers or field updates upon approval.
6. **Activate the Approval Process:**
   - Once configured, activate the approval process to start routing records for approval.

Using Flow Builder

Flow Builder allows you to create complex automations with conditional logic and user interactions. Here's how to get started with Flow Builder:

1. **Navigate to Flow Builder:**
   - From the Setup menu, type "Flow Builder" in the Quick Find box and select it.
2. **Create a New Flow:**
   - Click on the "New Flow" button and choose the type of flow you want to create (e.g., Screen Flow, Record-Triggered Flow).
3. **Add Elements:**
   - Drag and drop elements onto the canvas to build your flow. Elements can include screens, decisions, assignments, loops, and more.
4. **Configure Elements:**
   - Configure each element by setting properties and defining interactions. For example, you can create a decision element that branches the flow based on specific conditions.
5. **Save and Activate the Flow:**
   - Once your flow is configured, save and activate it to start automating your processes.

Best Practices for Workflow Automation

To make the most of workflow automation in Litify, consider the following best practices:

1. **Start Simple:**
   - Begin with simple automations and gradually add complexity as you become more comfortable with the tools.
2. **Test Thoroughly:**
   - Test all automated processes thoroughly to ensure they work as expected and do not cause unintended consequences.
3. **Document Your Workflows:**
   - Keep detailed documentation of all automated workflows, including criteria, actions, and expected outcomes. This helps with troubleshooting and future updates.
4. **Monitor and Optimize:**
   - Regularly monitor automated workflows to ensure they are functioning correctly. Optimize workflows based on feedback and changing business needs.

Conclusion

Congratulations on completing Chapter 8 of the Litify System Administrator Guide! You now have a comprehensive understanding of workflow automation within Litify. By leveraging tools such as Process Builder, Workflow Rules, Approval Processes, and Flow Builder, you can streamline your firm's processes and improve overall efficiency. In the next chapter, we will explore data management and import/export features, helping you to manage and utilize your data effectively. Happy automating!

Chapter 9: Data Management and Import/Export Features in Litify

Introduction

Welcome to Chapter 9 of the Litify System Administrator Guide! In this chapter, we will focus on data management and the import/export features within Litify. Proper data management is essential for maintaining the integrity and usability of your firm's information. By the end of this chapter, you will understand how to manage data effectively, import and export records, and utilize Litify's tools to keep your data organized and accessible.

Overview of Data Management

Data management in Litify involves organizing, storing, and maintaining data to ensure it is accurate, accessible, and secure. Key components of data management include:

- **Data Organization:** Structuring data in a logical and efficient manner.
- **Data Import:** Bringing external data into Litify.
- **Data Export:** Extracting data from Litify for use in other systems or for backup purposes.
- **Data Maintenance:** Regularly updating and cleaning data to maintain accuracy and relevance.

Organizing Data in Litify

Proper organization of data is crucial for efficient management. Here are some tips for organizing data in Litify:

1. **Use Custom Fields:**
   - Create custom fields to capture specific information relevant to your firm's processes. This ensures that all necessary data points are recorded and easily accessible.
2. **Implement Consistent Naming Conventions:**
   - Use consistent naming conventions for records, fields, and objects. This makes it easier to search for and identify data.
3. **Categorize Records:**
   - Utilize categories and tags to organize records. This helps in quickly filtering and retrieving specific sets of data.
4. **Utilize Record Types:**
   - Use record types to define different business processes and layouts for various records. This ensures that users see only the information relevant to their role.

Importing Data

Importing data into Litify is a common task when migrating from another system or adding new records. Here's how to import data effectively:

1. **Prepare Your Data:**
   - Ensure that your data is clean and well-organized before importing. Remove any duplicates and verify the accuracy of the information.
2. **Use Data Import Wizard:**
   - Litify provides a Data Import Wizard to facilitate the import process. To access it, navigate to the Setup menu, type "Data Import Wizard" in the Quick Find box, and select it.
3. **Choose the Data Type:**
   - Select the type of data you want to import (e.g., Accounts, Contacts, Cases). This helps the wizard map your data to the correct fields in Litify.
4. **Upload Your Data File:**
   - Upload your data file (typically in CSV format). The wizard will guide you through the process of mapping your file's columns to Litify fields.
5. **Map the Fields:**
   - Ensure that all columns in your data file are correctly mapped to the corresponding fields in Litify. This step is crucial for accurate data import.
6. **Start the Import:**
   - Once everything is mapped correctly, start the import process. The wizard will provide a summary of the import results, including any errors or warnings.

Exporting Data

Exporting data from Litify can be useful for reporting, analysis, or backup purposes. Here's how to export data:

1. **Navigate to Data Export:**
   - From the Setup menu, type "Data Export" in the Quick Find box and select "Data Export Service."
2. **Select Data to Export:**
   - Choose the objects and fields you want to export. You can select specific records or export all data for a particular object.
3. **Schedule Exports:**
   - Schedule regular data exports to ensure you have up-to-date backups. You can set the frequency (e.g., weekly, monthly) and choose to receive an email notification when the export is complete.
4. **Download Export Files:**
   - Once the export is complete, download the files from the provided link. The data will typically be in CSV format, which can be opened with spreadsheet software like Excel.

Maintaining Data Integrity

Maintaining data integrity is crucial for ensuring that your data remains accurate and reliable. Here are some best practices:

1. **Regular Data Cleaning:**
   - Periodically review and clean your data to remove duplicates, correct errors, and update outdated information.
2. **Validation Rules:**
   - Implement validation rules to enforce data quality. For example, you can require that certain fields be completed or that data follows a specific format.
3. **Audit Trails:**
   - Use audit trails to track changes to your data. This helps you monitor who made changes and when, which is important for maintaining accountability and data integrity.
4. **User Training:**
   - Train users on proper data entry practices to minimize errors and ensure consistency.

Best Practices for Data Management

To effectively manage data in Litify, consider the following best practices:

1. **Plan Your Data Strategy:**
   - Develop a clear data management strategy that outlines how data will be collected, organized, maintained, and used.
2. **Automate Where Possible:**
   - Use automation tools to reduce manual data entry and update tasks. This helps maintain data accuracy and saves time.
3. **Regular Backups:**
   - Regularly back up your data to prevent loss in case of system failures or other issues.
4. **Monitor Data Quality:**
   - Continuously monitor data quality and address any issues promptly to ensure the integrity of your data.

Conclusion

Congratulations on completing Chapter 9 of the Litify System Administrator Guide! You now have a comprehensive understanding of data management and the import/export features within Litify. By effectively organizing, importing, exporting, and maintaining your data, you can ensure that your firm's information is accurate, accessible, and secure. In the next chapter, we will explore customization and configuration, helping you tailor Litify to meet your firm's specific needs. Happy data managing!

Chapter 10: Customization and Configuration in Litify

Introduction

Welcome to Chapter 10 of the Litify System Administrator Guide! In this chapter, we will explore the customization and configuration options within Litify. Customizing Litify allows you to tailor the platform to meet your firm's specific needs and improve overall efficiency. By the end of this chapter, you will understand how to customize fields, layouts, and user interfaces, as well as configure settings to optimize Litify for your organization.

Overview of Customization and Configuration

Customization and configuration in Litify involve modifying the platform to suit your firm's unique workflows and requirements. Key areas include:

- **Custom Fields:** Adding and modifying fields to capture relevant data.
- **Page Layouts:** Customizing page layouts to improve user experience.
- **Record Types:** Defining different processes and layouts for various record types.
- **Lightning App Builder:** Creating custom apps and pages using the Lightning App Builder.
- **Configuration Settings:** Adjusting settings to optimize Litify's functionality.

Adding and Modifying Custom Fields

Custom fields allow you to capture specific information that is relevant to your firm's processes. Here's how to add and modify custom fields:

1. **Navigate to Object Manager:**
   - From the Setup menu, type "Object Manager" in the Quick Find box and select it.
2. **Select an Object:**
   - Choose the object you want to customize (e.g., Cases, Contacts).
3. **Create a New Field:**
   - Click on "Fields & Relationships" and then the "New" button to create a new custom field.
4. **Select Field Type:**
   - Choose the type of field you want to create (e.g., Text, Number, Date). Click "Next."
5. **Enter Field Details:**
   - Provide the necessary details for the field, such as Field Label, Field Name, and Description. Click "Next."
6. **Set Field-Level Security:**
   - Define the field-level security to control which profiles can view and edit the field. Click "Next."
7. **Add to Page Layouts:**

- Choose the page layouts where the field should be displayed. Click "Save" to create the field.

Customizing Page Layouts

Page layouts determine the arrangement of fields, related lists, and other elements on a record page. Here's how to customize page layouts:

1. **Navigate to Object Manager:**
   - From the Setup menu, type "Object Manager" in the Quick Find box and select it.
2. **Select an Object:**
   - Choose the object you want to customize (e.g., Cases, Contacts).
3. **Edit Page Layouts:**
   - Click on "Page Layouts" and select the layout you want to customize.
4. **Drag and Drop Elements:**
   - Use the drag-and-drop interface to add, remove, or rearrange fields, sections, and related lists. You can also add custom components and buttons.
5. **Save the Layout:**
   - Once you are satisfied with the changes, click "Save" to apply the customized layout.

Defining Record Types

Record types allow you to define different business processes and layouts for various types of records within the same object. Here's how to set up record types:

1. **Navigate to Object Manager:**
   - From the Setup menu, type "Object Manager" in the Quick Find box and select it.
2. **Select an Object:**
   - Choose the object you want to customize (e.g., Cases, Contacts).
3. **Create a New Record Type:**
   - Click on "Record Types" and then the "New" button to create a new record type.
4. **Enter Record Type Details:**
   - Provide the necessary details for the record type, such as Record Type Label and Record Type Name. Click "Next."
5. **Set Field-Level Security:**
   - Define the field-level security to control which profiles can view and edit the record type. Click "Next."
6. **Select Page Layouts:**
   - Choose the page layouts to be used for the record type. Click "Save" to create the record type.

Using Lightning App Builder

The Lightning App Builder allows you to create custom apps and pages using a drag-and-drop interface. Here's how to use it:

1. **Navigate to Lightning App Builder:**
   - From the Setup menu, type "Lightning App Builder" in the Quick Find box and select it.
2. **Create a New Page:**
   - Click on the "New" button and select the type of page you want to create (e.g., App Page, Home Page, Record Page).
3. **Add Components:**
   - Use the drag-and-drop interface to add components to the page. Components can include standard Salesforce components, custom components, and third-party components from the AppExchange.
4. **Configure Components:**
   - Configure the properties of each component to tailor its functionality to your needs.
5. **Save and Activate the Page:**
   - Once you are satisfied with the page, click "Save" and "Activate" to make it available to users.

Configuration Settings

Configuring settings allows you to optimize Litify's functionality for your organization. Here are some key settings to consider:

1. **General Settings:**
   - Adjust general settings such as language, time zone, and currency to match your firm's preferences.
2. **Email Settings:**
   - Configure email settings to ensure that all email communications are logged and tracked within Litify.
3. **Security Settings:**
   - Review and adjust security settings to protect sensitive information and control access to data.
4. **Data Management Settings:**
   - Set up data management settings, including data import/export preferences and data retention policies.

Best Practices for Customization and Configuration

To effectively customize and configure Litify, consider the following best practices:

1. **Plan Your Customizations:**

o   Develop a clear plan for customization, including which fields, layouts, and record types are needed. This helps ensure that customizations are purposeful and aligned with business needs.
2. **Test Customizations:**
   o   Test all customizations in a sandbox environment before applying them to your production instance. This helps identify and resolve any issues.
3. **Document Changes:**
   o   Keep detailed documentation of all customizations and configurations. This helps with troubleshooting and future updates.
4. **Train Users:**
   o   Provide training for users on how to use the customized features. This ensures that users can effectively leverage the customizations to improve their workflows.

Conclusion

Congratulations on completing Chapter 10 of the Litify System Administrator Guide! You now have a comprehensive understanding of customization and configuration within Litify. By tailoring fields, layouts, record types, and settings to your firm's specific needs, you can optimize the platform for maximum efficiency and usability. In the next chapter, we will explore advanced features and integrations, helping you to further enhance Litify's capabilities. Happy customizing!

Chapter 11: Advanced Features and Integrations in Litify

Introduction

Welcome to Chapter 11 of the Litify System Administrator Guide! In this chapter, we will explore the advanced features and integrations available within Litify. These tools can help you extend the functionality of Litify, integrate with other systems, and further optimize your workflows. By the end of this chapter, you will understand how to leverage advanced features and set up integrations to enhance your firm's capabilities.

Overview of Advanced Features and Integrations

Litify offers a range of advanced features and integrations to help you customize and extend the platform's functionality. Key areas include:

- **Custom Objects and Apps:** Create custom objects and applications tailored to your specific needs.
- **Integrations with Third-Party Tools:** Connect Litify with other software and tools your firm uses.
- **Litify Inbox:** Integrate email directly into Litify for seamless communication management.
- **API Access:** Use Litify's API to build custom integrations and automate processes.
- **AppExchange:** Leverage additional functionality by installing apps from the Salesforce AppExchange.

Creating Custom Objects and Apps

Custom objects and apps allow you to extend Litify's functionality to meet your firm's unique requirements. Here's how to create custom objects and apps:

1. **Navigate to Object Manager:**
   - From the Setup menu, type "Object Manager" in the Quick Find box and select it.
2. **Create a New Custom Object:**
   - Click on the "Create" button and select "Custom Object." Provide the necessary details, such as Object Name, Label, and Plural Label.
3. **Define Fields:**
   - Add custom fields to your object to capture the necessary data. Follow the same steps outlined in Chapter 10 for creating custom fields.
4. **Set Page Layouts:**
   - Customize the page layouts for your custom object to ensure that users can easily view and interact with the data.
5. **Create a Custom App:**

- From the Setup menu, type "App Manager" in the Quick Find box and select it. Click "New Lightning App" to create a new custom app. Add your custom object and any other necessary components to the app.

Integrating with Third-Party Tools

Litify can integrate with a variety of third-party tools to streamline your workflows. Here are some common integrations:

1. **Document Management Systems:**
   - Integrate with tools like DocuSign or Adobe Sign for electronic signatures. Visit the Salesforce AppExchange to find and install the appropriate integration package.
2. **Billing and Accounting Software:**
   - Connect Litify with billing and accounting software like QuickBooks or Xero to automate financial processes. Use the AppExchange to find compatible integrations.
3. **Marketing Automation:**
   - Integrate with marketing automation tools like HubSpot or Mailchimp to manage client communication and marketing campaigns. Install the integration packages from the AppExchange.

Using Litify Inbox

Litify Inbox is an email integration tool that brings your email into Litify, allowing for seamless communication management. Here's how to set up and use Litify Inbox:

1. **Install Litify Inbox:**
   - From the Setup menu, type "AppExchange" in the Quick Find box and select it. Search for "Litify Inbox" and follow the instructions to install the package.
2. **Configure Email Settings:**
   - Navigate to the Litify Inbox settings and connect your email account. Follow the prompts to grant Litify access to your email.
3. **Using Litify Inbox:**
   - Once set up, you can send and receive emails directly within Litify. Emails are automatically logged to the relevant records, making it easy to track all client communications.

Accessing Litify's API

Litify's API allows you to build custom integrations and automate processes by interacting with Litify data programmatically. Here's how to get started with the API:

1. **Generate API Credentials:**

- From the Setup menu, type "API" in the Quick Find box and select "API Access." Generate the necessary API credentials, including the client ID and client secret.
2. **Use API Documentation:**
   - Visit the Salesforce API documentation to learn how to make API calls, authenticate, and interact with Litify data.
3. **Build Custom Integrations:**
   - Use the API to build custom integrations that automate processes, such as syncing data between Litify and other systems, creating custom reports, or triggering actions based on specific events.

Leveraging the AppExchange

The Salesforce AppExchange is a marketplace where you can find and install apps to extend the functionality of Litify. Here's how to leverage the AppExchange:

1. **Browse the AppExchange:**
   - From the Setup menu, type "AppExchange" in the Quick Find box and select it. Browse the available apps by category, such as document management, marketing, or billing.
2. **Install Apps:**
   - Select the apps that meet your needs and follow the installation instructions. Most apps offer free trials, so you can test them before committing.
3. **Manage Installed Apps:**
   - After installing an app, navigate to the "Installed Packages" section in Setup to manage and configure the app settings.

Best Practices for Advanced Features and Integrations

To effectively utilize advanced features and integrations in Litify, consider the following best practices:

1. **Plan Integrations Carefully:**
   - Plan your integrations to ensure they align with your firm's workflows and do not introduce unnecessary complexity.
2. **Test Integrations:**
   - Test all integrations in a sandbox environment before deploying them to production. This helps identify and resolve any issues.
3. **Monitor Performance:**
   - Regularly monitor the performance of integrations to ensure they are functioning correctly and efficiently.
4. **Document Customizations:**
   - Keep detailed documentation of all customizations and integrations. This aids in troubleshooting and future updates.
5. **Provide Training:**

- Train users on how to use new features and integrations effectively. This ensures they can leverage the full capabilities of the platform.

Conclusion

Congratulations on completing Chapter 11 of the Litify System Administrator Guide! You now have a comprehensive understanding of advanced features and integrations within Litify. By leveraging custom objects, integrating with third-party tools, using Litify Inbox, accessing the API, and installing apps from the AppExchange, you can extend Litify's functionality to meet your firm's unique needs. In the next chapter, we will explore best practices for ongoing system administration and maintenance. Happy integrating!

Chapter 12: Best Practices for Ongoing System Administration and Maintenance in Litify

Introduction

Welcome to Chapter 12 of the Litify System Administrator Guide! In this final chapter, we will discuss best practices for ongoing system administration and maintenance. Maintaining your Litify environment ensures that your system remains efficient, secure, and up-to-date. By the end of this chapter, you will understand how to perform regular maintenance tasks, monitor system performance, and implement best practices to keep your Litify environment running smoothly.

Importance of Ongoing Maintenance

Regular maintenance is crucial for ensuring the long-term success of your Litify implementation. It helps prevent system issues, maintains data integrity, and ensures that your firm can continue to operate efficiently. Key areas of focus include:

- **System Performance:** Monitoring and optimizing system performance to ensure fast and reliable access to Litify.
- **Data Integrity:** Regularly cleaning and updating data to maintain accuracy and relevance.
- **Security:** Ensuring that your system remains secure and compliant with industry standards.
- **User Training:** Keeping users informed and trained on best practices and new features.

Regular Maintenance Tasks

Performing regular maintenance tasks helps keep your Litify environment in top shape. Here are some essential tasks to include in your maintenance routine:

1. **Data Backup:**
   - Schedule regular backups of your data to prevent loss in case of system failures or other issues. Store backups in a secure location and test the restoration process periodically.
2. **Data Cleaning:**
   - Regularly review and clean your data to remove duplicates, correct errors, and update outdated information. Use tools like data validation rules and duplicate management to assist with this process.
3. **System Updates:**
   - Stay up-to-date with the latest Litify and Salesforce updates. Regularly check for new releases and apply updates to ensure you have the latest features and security patches.
4. **User Account Management:**

- Regularly review user accounts to ensure that access levels are appropriate and up-to-date. Deactivate accounts for users who no longer need access and update roles and permissions as needed.
5. **Audit Logs:**
   - Monitor audit logs to track changes to your data and system configurations. This helps maintain accountability and identify any unauthorized access or unusual activity.

Monitoring System Performance

Monitoring system performance helps ensure that your Litify environment remains fast and reliable. Here are some strategies for effective performance monitoring:

1. **Dashboard and Reports:**
   - Create dashboards and reports to monitor key performance metrics, such as system usage, data volume, and response times. Regularly review these reports to identify and address any performance issues.
2. **Salesforce Optimizer:**
   - Use the Salesforce Optimizer tool to analyze your system and receive recommendations for improving performance. This tool helps identify areas where you can optimize configurations and streamline processes.
3. **System Limits:**
   - Monitor system limits, such as API usage and data storage limits, to ensure that you stay within allowable thresholds. Set up alerts to notify you when limits are approaching.
4. **Performance Testing:**
   - Conduct regular performance testing to evaluate the speed and responsiveness of your system. Use tools like Salesforce Performance Testing to simulate user activity and identify bottlenecks.

Ensuring Security and Compliance

Maintaining security and compliance is essential for protecting sensitive information and meeting industry standards. Here are some best practices for ensuring security:

1. **Access Controls:**
   - Implement strong access controls to ensure that only authorized users can access sensitive data. Use profiles, roles, and permission sets to define access levels.
2. **Two-Factor Authentication (2FA):**
   - Enable two-factor authentication for added security. This requires users to provide a second form of verification, such as a code sent to their phone, when logging in.
3. **Regular Security Audits:**

- Conduct regular security audits to evaluate your system's security posture. Identify and address any vulnerabilities or areas of concern.

4. **Compliance Checks:**
   - Ensure that your system complies with industry standards and regulations, such as GDPR or HIPAA. Implement policies and procedures to maintain compliance and document your efforts.

Keeping Users Informed and Trained

Keeping users informed and trained on best practices and new features helps ensure that they can effectively use Litify. Here are some strategies for ongoing user training:

1. **Training Sessions:**
   - Conduct regular training sessions to keep users updated on new features, best practices, and system updates. Use a mix of in-person training, webinars, and online tutorials.
2. **User Guides and Documentation:**
   - Provide users with comprehensive guides and documentation to help them navigate the system and perform their tasks. Update these resources regularly to reflect changes and new features.
3. **Feedback Mechanisms:**
   - Establish feedback mechanisms, such as surveys and user groups, to gather input from users. Use this feedback to identify areas for improvement and address any issues.
4. **Support Resources:**
   - Ensure that users know how to access support resources, such as help desks and knowledge bases. Provide clear instructions for reporting issues and requesting assistance.

Best Practices for Ongoing System Administration

To effectively manage your Litify environment, consider the following best practices:

1. **Proactive Maintenance:**
   - Adopt a proactive approach to system maintenance by regularly reviewing and updating configurations, monitoring performance, and addressing issues before they become critical.
2. **Documentation:**
   - Maintain detailed documentation of all system configurations, customizations, and maintenance activities. This helps with troubleshooting and future updates.
3. **Collaboration:**
   - Collaborate with other system administrators, users, and stakeholders to ensure that your system meets the needs of your firm. Regularly communicate with these groups to gather input and share updates.
4. **Continuous Improvement:**

- Continuously evaluate and improve your system administration practices. Stay informed about new features, tools, and best practices to keep your Litify environment optimized.

Conclusion

Congratulations on completing Chapter 12 of the Litify System Administrator Guide! You now have a comprehensive understanding of best practices for ongoing system administration and maintenance. By performing regular maintenance tasks, monitoring system performance, ensuring security and compliance, and keeping users informed and trained, you can ensure that your Litify environment remains efficient, secure, and up-to-date. Thank you for following this guide, and happy administrating!